Black book of isometric powerlifting

First words:

This small book is intended to inform and entertain, but mostly inform. If you are unable to get to a gym with barbell or nautilus-type machines, and even ultra-heavy adjustable dumbbells are unavailable to you, or someone you know and care for, then this book is for you.

This small volume is then presented as factual knowlegde to be passed on. How to powerlift using only sneaker-shoes, a towel, a wall, a doorframe.

If performed correctly, as described herein, these exercises are safe and extremely potent. You will potentially build both tendon-strength and size.

The only reasons you could have not to do these isometric power-builders would be if you have an injured spine, disc-prolapse or scoliosis.

If you are physically healthy and follow the instructions to the word you will be strong.

!

Survival strength:

I won't describe it in close detail, but the time came when I was arrested, something like a dozen policemen with guns and clubs and shields, and they performed a complete home-invasion and took me away.

I was then locked up and moved between a couple of facilities. It then turned out that I would be attacked by psychos inside, no one there to help me. I was kept from training opportunities and starved.

When I contacted external and higher authorities I was released from one day to the next. But I had spent 3 months starving, being bullied, ridiculed, even attempted killed.

This sprouted a seed I already carried in my heart. I, like so many other men, wanted to be strong, fit, toned, cut, ripped, shredded and muscular. Who doesn't?

The difference was that now I had experienced being outnumbered and accused. Attacked. Now I had a reason. So I found out how.

!

Powerlifting versus isometric contraction:

The way I would do powerlifting for strenght and mass, would be to either load an adjustable barbell or adjustable dumbbells, and then perform a set of 3 basic exercises with a challenging weight.

First the deadlift, weights on the ground, being lifted with perfect form. 3-6 repetitions.

Then the front-squats. Clean the bell(s) to rest with your grip on protruding shoulders, and then squat with perfect form, 5-12 repetitions.

Last the standing press. From shoulder-level to straight arms. 3-6 repetitions.

The weight-load will then have to be decreased between each exercise to fit the way physical strenght is distributed in the human body.

You would need to do from 1 to 3 sets total this way.

The isometric power-lifting in this book is what is technically known as 'overcoming isometrics'. That term basically means that you are pushing and pulling against imovable objects. This can build strength in your entire body, just like training with challenging weights.

I will outline the perfect technique to be used to keep you safe.

There are not 3 but 4 overcoming isometric contractions that I want you to perform. These will cover your entire body and could also be described as 'compound exercises', and that mean they all hit more than one muscle-group at once.

Lastly there is one 'yielding isometric' exercise that you must also do. yielding isometrics means that you hold a position against gravity for a long as you can with correct form.

It is important that you perform all the pushes and pulls, and in the given order. It is equally important that you follow the words on correct technique to the letter.

!

Safety first:

Spinal health is a primary concern when doing compound pulling-type contractions. You **must** keep your spine as straight as possible. This also goes for the pushing-type contractions I will describe.

Breathing has vital importance to your health as well. You **must** do 'valve-breathing'. This term means that you first inhale untill your lungs are full, but at a comfortable level of expansion, and then release air through your mouth preferably, as though you are giving off steam through a valve. This must be done for the duration of each contraction. It will keep the internal pressure that will build from getting to your head.

Finally you **must** complete the power-exercises with the final 'yielding-type' exercise. For your posture, abs and physical balance.

The black book

Correct technique:

You must perform 1-3 sets consisting of the 4 power-exercises in the given order. You must perform each exercise once, then move on to the next. You must end the sets with 'the plank'.

Each power-exercise must take 5 seconds to complete. You will simply count to 5 in your head. You will start the contractions gradually, then move to full force, then let it go, all within 5 seconds.

You must inhale first, while adapting to the correct stance, then exhale through your mouth during the contraction, as though letting out steam through a valve. You must also mentally try to keep the internal pressure in your abdomen.

The power-exercises are as follow:

1: isometric deadlift

2: isometric chest-press

3: isometric biceps-pull

4: isometric shoulder-press

Iso deadlift

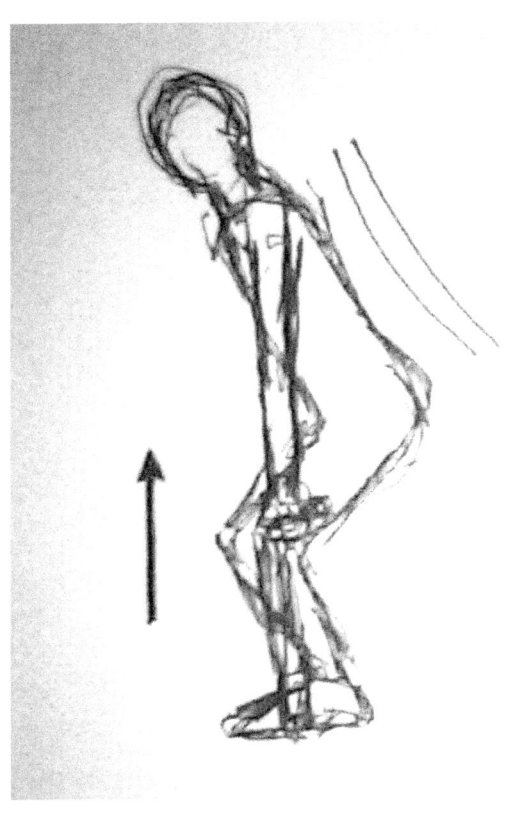

Iso chest-press

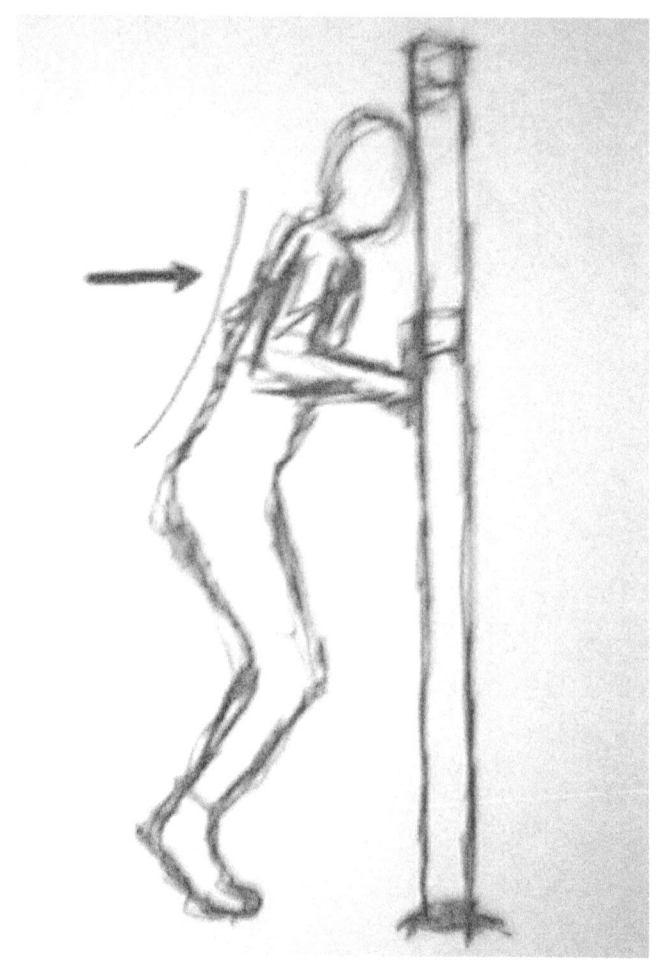

Iso biceps-pull

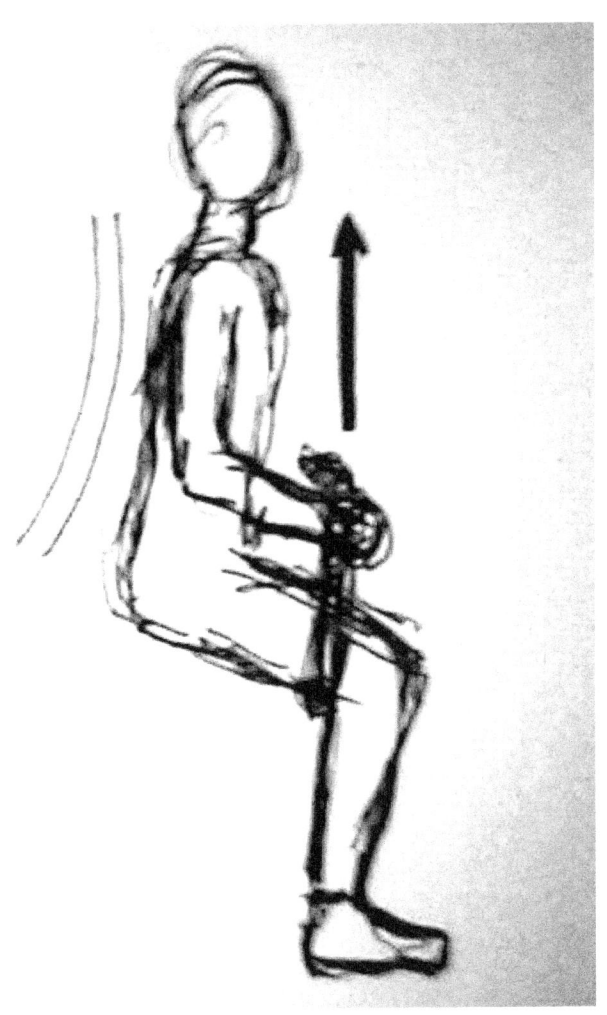

Iso shoulder-press

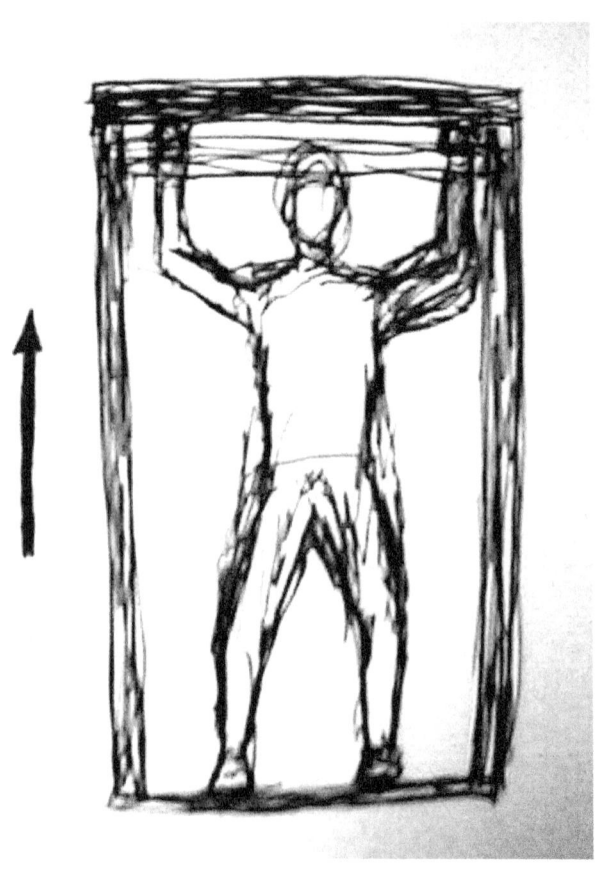

You **must** wear shoes to perform the deadlift.

You will fold a cloth-towel the long way, stand on it with middle foot position, bend slightly to get into deadlift-position (but a deadlift is not a squat). You must then grab the towel on the ends, as high or low as it fits you.

You **must** have perfect symmetry in your grip, that means your hands must be in exactly parallel height.

You **must** keep your back straight.

You must bend in at the knees to perform the chest-press against a wall, or with your hands on each side of a doorframe. You must bend the knees to spread the contraction to you thighs and calves. This is important to spread the effects of the workout to all central muscles and keep things as 'compound' as possible.

You must use the folded towel again for the third exercise, and squat down until your thighs are about parallel to the floor, then place the towel under your knees. You then pull for your biceps and lattissimus dorsi/upper back.

You must stand in a doorframe for the final exercise. You must bend slightly in the knees, place your hands on the top-bar and press. It it a good idea to wear shoes for this as well.

Even out the load:

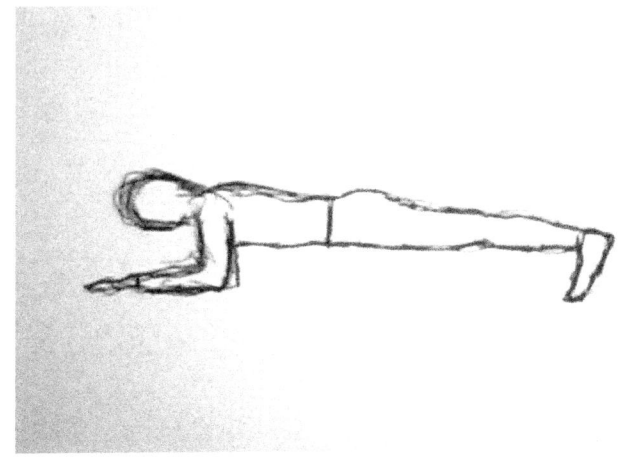

The final exercise I give you is as important as the previous 4.

This is the plank. You must rest on the toes of your feet and your hands and elbows and keep the back straight. You should just breathe freely when doing this.

This is to train your abs and even out the load on your body, for the sake of your posture.

When you have performed 1 to 3 sets of the first 4 exercises, you should do the plank once, and try to hold it for as long as you can. At least 20-30 seconds.

!

I want you to follow the directions to the letter, exactly as described and with the exercises in the given order.

!

How often should you train?

This will just come from my own experience: you must train more than once per week. Training only once per week or even less increases your chance of injury. This doesn't just go for powerlifting, but for all types of exercise, including running.

Training twice weekly will give you some initial results, and will maintain a certain level of fitness or strength.

You can easily adapt to training every day, once or even twice, such as AM and PM. If doing things that way you should go by how you feel. If you're already worn out then rest.

You can always have a resting day or two if need be.

Can you both powerlift and do cardio?

My experience: yes, you can both strength-train and do running or other forms of cardio.

You will need to do ultra-running (longer than marathon distance) to loose muscle.

But if you want to be strong you should frequently build up and preserve energy for your strength-training.

You are what you eat:

My hard-earned experience: you should not drink protein-shakes from powder. It is useless. Your body can not absorb those amounts of protein if you are not on some kind of anabolic steroids, and some of that protein will then be distributed out with your urine, possibly wearing out your kidneys over the years.

You should not take creatine supplements in any form. Creatine phosphate is generated by your own liver when you eat protein, and the meat of all vertebrates contains creatine phosphate, as does cow-milk.

It is often said of pro power-lifters that they will eat much. Many of them obviously do. You should just eat like your body tells you. Junk food makes you stronger.

If you want to loose weight you should try to loose fat and not muscle. It is mainly your diet that will allow this process.

My advice: don't go on a low carb diet. It

really feels bad, physically and mentally. Rather, if you really want to loose weight try intermittent fasting. For instance you could just not eat after 20:00 in the evening, and not eat again until 16:00 the next day. Try that twice a week on not adjoining days while keeping up with your training.

Where ever you are, and for whatever reason you needed my advice, I hope the best for you.

Freedom is not just another word for nothing left to lose.

Printed in Great Britain
by Amazon